D0345262

DON'TS
FOR WIVES

BY

BLANCHE EBBUTT

LONDON
A. & C. BLACK, LTD.
1913

PREFACE

Art is a hard mistress, and there is no art quite so hard as that of being a wife.

So many women exhaust their artistic power in getting married, which is, after all, a comparatively easy business. It takes a perfect artist to remain married – married in the perfect sense of the term; but most of us have to be content to muddle through.

Imagine a girl called upon without a single lesson to produce a tune – a lot of tunes – in fact, one never-ending succession of harmonies – from the most difficult instrument in the world. Note that the instrument not only gets

grumpy in cold weather and skittish in
the spring – not only slacks or breaks
its strings with every change of tem-
perature – but becomes tempestuous
over a tight shoe, broody over an out-of-
date egg, and cross, sulky, or mirthful
for reasons that no sane woman can
understand.

That is what the average wife has to
reckon with; and if she intends to play
the game – humiliating as some may
think it – HE will loom largely on the
horizon all her life.

I hope she may find it worthwhile to
take a few hints from an old hand.

BLANCHE EBBUTT.

DON'TS FOR WIVES

I.—PERSONALITIES.

DON'T think that there is any satisfactory substitute for love between husband and wife. Respect and esteem make a good foundation, but they won't do alone.

Don't be surprise, if you have married for money, or position, or fame, that you get *only* money, or position, or fame; love cannot be bought.

Don't think that, because you have married for love, you can never know a moment's unhappiness. Life is not a bed of roses, but love will help to extract the thorns.

Don't expect life to be all sunshine. Besides, if there are no clouds, you will lose the opportunity of showing your husband what a good chum you can be.

Don't look at the black side of the cloud. It is only a shadow cast by the silver lining.

Don't lose heart when life seems hard. Look forward to the corner you are bound to turn soon, and point it out to your husband.

Don't moralise by way of winning back the love that seems to be waning. Make yourself extra charming and arrange delicious dinners which include all your husband's favourite dishes.

Don't put showy qualities before honesty and uprightness in your husband.

Don't despise sound common sense because he doesn't indulge in brilliant inspirations.

Don't expect your husband to have all the feminine virtues as well as all the masculine ones. There would be nothing left for *you* if your other half were such a paragon.

Don't be troubled because your husband is not an Adonis. Beauty is only skin deep and the cleverest men are rarely the handsomest, judged by ordinary standards.

Don't worry about little faults in your husband which merely amused you in your lover. If they were not important then, they are not important now. Besides, what about yours?

Don't put on airs with your husband. If you can't be natural with him, you shouldn't have married him.

Don't expect your husband to be an angel. You would get very tired of him if he were.

Don't boast of your husband's money or birth or cleverness to your friends. It is nearly as bad as boasting of your own.

Don't tell all your women friends of your husband's faults, but—

Don't din his perfections into the ears of every woman you meet. Be satisfied to enjoy them.

Don't interpret too literally the 'obey' of the Marriage Service. Your husband has no right to control your individuality.

Don't be discontented and think your husband not 'manly' because he happens to be short and thin, and not very strong. Manliness is not a purely physical quality.

Don't take your husband at his own valuation, but at yours. He may be unduly modest, or just a little too cock-sure.

Don't expect a man to see everything

from a woman's point of view. Try to put yourself in his place for a change.

Don't advise your husband on subjects of which you are, if anything, rather more ignorant than he.

Don't try to model your husband on some other woman's husband. Let him be himself and make the best of him.

Don't let your husband feel that you are a 'dear little woman', but no good intellectually. If you find yourself getting stale, wake up your brain. Let there be nothing your husband can talk about that you will be unable to understand.

Don't profess to care nothing about politics. Any man who is worth his salt does care, and many men learn to despise women as a whole because their wives take such an unintelligent attitude.

Don't set your husband up on a pedestal and then cry when you find that he is only an ordinary man, after all.

Don't be talked down by your husband when you want to express your views on any subject. You have a right to be heard.

Don't be rude to people whom you dislike, or your husband will have just cause to be ashamed of you. Politeness costs nothing.

Don't expect to know your husband inside and out within a month of marriage. For a long time you will be making discoveries; file them for future reference.

Don't vegetate as you grow older if you happen to live in the country. Some women are like cows, but there is really no need to stagnate. Keep both brain and body on the move.

Don't consent to be treated as a child who cannot be expected to take any responsibility. Insist on hearing bad news as well as good. You did not marry your husband to be wrapped in cotton wool and put away in a glass case; you married him to be the partner of his joys and sorrows.

Don't omit to pay your husband an occasional compliment. If he looks nice as he comes in dressed for the opera, tell him so. If he has been successful with his chickens, or his garden, or his photography, compliment him on his results. Don't let him have to fall back on self-esteem all the while for want of a little well-directed praise.

Don't pose as a helpless creature who can do nothing for herself; don't drag your husband away from his office to see you across a street; don't profess to be unable to understand Bradshaw, or to take a journey alone. It is true that the weak, clinging wife is often a favourite, but she is equally often a nuisance.

Don't live on top of a spiritual mountain. Try to be

"a creature
Not too bright and good,
For human nature's daily food,"

As Wordsworth has it.

Don't forget to wish your husband good-morning when he sets off to the office. He will feel the lack of your good-bye kiss all day.

Don't brood; that way madness lies. Don't hesitate, if you catch yourself brooding, to 'take a day off' in the best way you can. Go out and gossip with your friend; get to a theatre where there is a play that will make you laugh; or try a concert or a cinema show – anything that will take you out of yourself. Take the brooding habit in time before it gets too strong a hold of you.

Don't stop at that. Half the brooding and half the ill-humour in the world are due to foolish feeding. The woman who broods probably does not trouble about the meals when her husband is away – doesn't have a decent repast at midday, but some bread and butter, or pastries and a cup of tea; or perhaps she eats too much meat. Three, or even two, meat meals a day tend to make the world look very black to the middle aged. The ever-flowing teapot is as bad.

II.—HOW TO AVOID DISCORD.

Don't expect to drop into matrimonial harmony with the end of the honeymoon; you have not thoroughly learned to know each other's foibles by that time.

Don't expect all the love to be on his

side. It will wear thin for lack of support if you do.

Don't quarrel with your husband. Remember it takes two to make a quarrel; don't you be one of them. Lovers' quarrels may be all very well, but matrimonial doses are apt to leave a bitter flavour behind. The quarrels of spouses are not always the renewal of love.

Don't say, 'I told you so,' to your husband, however much you feel tempted to. It does no good, and he will be grateful to you for *not* saying it.

Don't expect your husband to make *you* happy while you are simply a passive agent. Do your best to make *him* happy and you will find happiness yourself.

Don't nag your husband. If he won't carry out your wishes for love of you, he certainly won't because you nag him.

Don't sulk with your husband. If he has annoyed you about something, 'get it off your chest.' A sulky wife is as bad as a termagant.

Don't tread on your husband's (metaphorical) pet corns. There are plenty of other people who will do that. *You* needn't help.

Don't think you can each go your own way and be as happy as if you pulled in double harness. In all important matters you want to pull together.

Don't expect all the 'give' to be on his side, and all the 'take' on yours.

Don't argue with a stubborn husband. Drop the matter before argument leads to temper. You can generally gain your point in some other way.

Don't 'manage' your husband too visibly. Of course, he may require the most careful management, but you don't want your friends to think of him as a hen-pecked husband. Above all, never let him think you manage him.

Don't wash your dirty linen in public, or even before your most intimate friends. If there are certain disagreeable matters to discuss, take care to discuss them in complete privacy.

Don't go to sleep feeling cross with your husband. If he has annoyed you during the evening, forgive him and close your eyes at peace with him. 'Let not the sun go down upon your wrath' is a very good motto.

Don't return to an old grievance. Once the matter has been thrashed out, let it be forgotten, or at least never allude to it again.

Don't be too proud to seek a reconciliation if you have unhappily quarrelled with your husband. Never mind if you think he was to blame—give him half a chance, and he will probably own up to it; but he may not care to take the first step, lest he be repulsed.

Don't refuse to give way about trifles. When a principle is at stake, it is a different matter, but most matrimonial differences arise from trifles.

Don't say bitter things when you are angry. They not only sting at the time, but they eat their way in and are remembered long after *you* have forgotten them.

Don't keep your sweetest smiles and your best manners for outsiders; let your husband come first.

Don't believe that marriage is a lottery over which you have no control. If you and your husband have both married for love, the lottery is really a 'dead cert'.

Don't attempt to dictate to your husband on any subject. He won't stand it, and there will be trouble. But—

Don't let him dictate to you. Always respond to reasonable persuasion, but let him see that, although you are willing to be led, you are not to be driven.

Don't cease to be lovers because you are married. There is no need for the honeymoon to come to an end while you live.

Don't let your husband feel that you are always criticising everything he does. Leave the role of critic to others. This does not mean that you are to give no friendly criticism. There is a happy medium between constant carping and fulsome flattery which you should seek.

Don't snub your husband. Nothing is more unpleasant for lookers-on than to hear a snub administered by a wife, and it is more than unpleasant for the husband; it is degrading.

Don't ever seem to join forces with those who criticise your husband, even in the length of his moustache or the cut of his hair. He is more sensitive to his little vanities than in his big exploits. The great man will be modest enough about his world-shaking inventions; but if you jibe at the colour of his eyes, you have him on the raw.

Don't forget that you and your husband are a partnership. If he thinks his partner is against him, to whom can he look for sympathy? If YOU join in the world's opposition, he may feel that he is a very Ishmael, and become one, in truth.

III.—HABITS.

Don't be everlastingly trying to change your husband's habits, unless they are *very* bad ones. Take him as you find him, and leave him at peace.

Don't grumble because his idea of work differs from yours. If he works hard at anything, let him do it in his own way, and be satisfied.

Don't grudge your husband his little luxuries—his cigarette, or his pipes, or his books. Who has a better right to them than the man who earns them?

Don't try to wean him from any pet hobby he may have because his things are always about, or because it is such a messy occupation. Let him be as messy as he likes in his own home—only give him plenty of space for his fads, and he won't want to carry them into the living rooms; in fact he would much rather not, lest sacrilegious hands should touch his treasures.

Don't hesitate to inconvenience yourself to give him a den all his own. He's really a good fellow, and a lot of his worries will melt away if he has a place to himself for a while. When he is out, the den will be yours.

Don't say you can't allow smoking in your drawing room, or else don't expect your husband to sit in it. Let his home be Liberty Hall in every respect.

Don't claim to read all your husband's correspondence. Probably he would not have the slightest objection to your doing so if you did not make a point of it.

Don't let your husband expect to read all *your* correspondence as a matter of course. Each should respect the other's privacy.

Don't check your husband's high spirits. Let him sing at the top of his voice in the bathroom, or whistle out of tune on the stairs, and be thankful for a cheerful man about the house.

Don't become a mere echo of your husband. If you never hold an opinion of your own about anything, life will be dreadfully colourless for both of you, and there will be nothing to talk about. Remember that variety is the spice of life, and that the sweetest of echoes is apt to become monotonous.

Don't let your husband sharpen lead pencils all over your drawing-room carpet. He will be none the happier for it, and the carpet will suffer as well as the maid's temper. He doesn't do it out of pure cussedness; it is mere thoughtlessness, and a little instruction will induce him to use the hearth or the waste-paper basket. But don't 'row' him; be good-natured about it. After all, most husbands are only grown-up children in such matters.

Don't encourage your husband to drop, when alone with you, the little courtesies he would show to other women. You are not the *least* important of women to him.

Don't spend half the morning in bed because there is "nothing to get up for."

The day is not long enough for all the things you might do if you liked.

Don't let your husband make you selfish, and don't you make him selfish. If there is one specially comfortable chair that you both like, don't let him always put you into it, and don't persuade him always to sit in it himself. Turn and turn about is a very good rule.

Don't open the door for yourself when your husband is present. He would open it for a lady guest, let him open it for you. Besides, your boys will not learn the little courtesies that count nearly so well by precept as by example.

Don't work yourself into a fever every time your husband omits to turn up

at the expected time.   He is in all
probability neither run over by a motor-
car, nor robbed and murdered on his
way home, nor lying in a lonely land
with a sprained ankle, nor in any other
of the terrible predicaments your
imagination pictures.   Probably he
stopped at the bookstall to buy an
evening paper, and so missed his train.
So don't greet him hysterically when he
does arrive.

Don't think it beneath you to put
your husband's slippers ready for him.
On a cold evening, especially, it makes
all the difference to his comfort if the
soles are warmed through.

IV.—FINANCIAL MATTERS.

Don't think money makes happiness. It helps to procure comfort, but true happiness lies deeper than that.

Don't be satisfied to let your husband work overtime to earn money for frocks for you. Manage with fewer frocks.

Don't get into debt if you can possibly help it. You don't want to carry a load around on your own mind, nor to worry your husband with it.

Don't spend every penny you get, unless it is so little that you absolutely must. Try to put by for the proverbial "rainy day."

Don't expect to begin where your

parents left off. A little struggle in your early married life won't hurt you.

Don't spend your life keeping up appearances. Why should you buy expensive furniture for the benefit of your neighbours if you haven't a balance at the bank?

Don't entrench on your little capital every time you think you would like something which you haven't got. You won't find it so easy to replace these sums as your necessary expenses grow.

Don't have any secrets from your husband in financial matters. Complete confidence is best.

Don't let him have any financial secrets from you. You are partners, and you have as much right to know what is the balance at the bank as he has.

Don't spend all the best years of your life pinching and saving unnecessarily, until you are too old to get any pleasure out of your money.

Don't pile up money for your children. Give them the best education possible, and let them make their own way.

Don't urge your husband to save enough money to "retire." His retirement may very likely shorten his life by depriving him of its chief interest.

Don't exercise your passion for
economy on your husband's linen.
Don't expect him to wear his shirts and
collars twice because the laundry bill is
so high, and don't grudge him a couple
of handkerchiefs a day. If necessary,
you can wash these yourself. Anyhow,
rather economise on your own or the
household washing.

Don't consent to let your husband pay
all the wages and tradesmen's books and
your dress bills, and then say there is
nothing for which you need money.
Some wives have to ask their husbands
for every halfpenny stamp they want;
not because money is scarce, but
because their husbands like to feel their
power. Don't let yours begin it.

Don't forget that you have a right to some money to spend as you like; you earn it as wife, and mother, and house-keeper. Very likely you will spend it on the house or the children when you get it; but that doesn't matter—it is yours to spend as you like.

Don't impose on your husband's good nature. Because he is 'such a dear,' and will give you anything you like to ask for, don't take advantage and ask for something unreasonable.

Don't grudge the trouble of keeping accounts. It is worth while knowing what becomes of your money.

Don't hesitate to plan out large expenditures with your husband. Usually a woman is very good at small economics, but often a man has a better grip of essentials in spending large amounts.

Don't run up big bills at a number of shops and then find it necessary to go to your husband to help you out. Try to know where you are all the time.

Don't confuse stinginess with economy. You can be careful without being mean.

Don't object to your husband's life insurance. He will die none the sooner because his life is insured, and if you should unfortunately have to end your life without him, it may be a great help to you.

V.—EVENINGS AT HOME.

Don't be out if you can help it when your husband gets home after his day's work.

Don't let him have to search the house for you. Listen for his latch-key and meet him on the threshold.

Don't omit the kiss of greeting. It cheers a man when he is tired to feel that his wife is glad to see him home.

Don't greet him at the door with a catalogue of the dreadful crimes committed by servants during the day.

Don't think your husband horrid if he seems a bit irritable; probably he has had a very trying day, and his nerves are overwrought.

Don't forget if he is 'nervy' to watch if the tea habit is getting too strong in him. Nerves are often due to too much tea as to too much worry.

Don't bother your husband with a stream of senseless chatter if you can see that he is very fatigued. Help him to the tit-bits at dinner; modulate your voice; don't remark on his silence. If you have any cheery little anecdote to relate, tell it with quiet humour, and by-and-by he will respond. But if you tackle him in the wrong way, the two of you will spend a miserable evening.

Don't 'fuss' your husband. Mistaken attentions often annoy a man dreadfully. If he comes home late after a busy day, and has a quiet little supper alone he doesn't want you to jump up like a Jack-in-the-box with 'would you like more pepper, darling?' and present him with the cruet from the opposite end of the table, when he already has one in front of him. See that everything is conveniently placed for him and then leave the man alone until he has fed. Let him feel your sympathetic presence near him, but occupy yourself in reading or doing needlework; anyhow, don't 'fuss' him.

Don't spend all your time with the children, and leave none over for your husband. You can have them during the day; it is your husband's turn when he comes home in the evening.

Don't nauseate your husband with talking 'baby' *all* the time. As baby's father, he will stand a good deal of it, but remember that there are other interests in the world.

Don't get the idea that all your husband wants is a housekeeper, or a decorative head of the table. He wants a companion and when he is at home he doesn't want you to be always somewhere else.

Don't choose the very time your husband is at home to 'see about' all sorts of things in other parts of the house. Sit with him by the fire; smoke with him if it pleases you and him; read or be read to; sing or play cards with him, or chat with him about anything

that interests him. It is your business
to keep him amused in the evening.

Don't say you don't want to be both-
ered with business details.   By all
means encourage your husband to put
business worries behind him, but some-
times he can do that best by telling
them to you.

Don't tell your husband of every
petty annoyance and pin-prick you have
suffered from during the day, but *do* tell
him your real troubles; he expects to
share them, and his advice may help
you.   In any case, his sympathy will
halve the trouble.

Don't be shy of showing your love.
Don't expect him to take it for granted.
A playful caress as you pass his chair,

an unexpected touch on the shoulder, makes all the difference between merely *knowing* that you care for him and actually *feeling* it.

Don't expect your husband to want to spend evenings at home if you don't make home the most comfortable place. Don't stuff your drawing room with priceless knick knacks that he will knock over when he stretches out his hand for an ash tray. Don't have chairs that look nice but are not comfortable to sit in, nor cushions that may only be looked at. It is a mistake to suppose that a man likes best the home of the 'pattern' housekeeper. He doesn't; it makes him want to kick things about.

Don't sit and yawn while your husband is smoking his last pipe, or finishing his novel or his game of patience. And don't mutely reproach him by going to sleep in an armchair. If you are too tired to stay up decently, go to bed, but don't try to hurry your husband off before he is ready.

Don't refuse to see your husband's jokes. They may be pretty poor ones, but it won't hurt you to smile at them.

Don't be too serious and heavy at home. Make things bright for your husband.

Don't grumble because your husband insists on wearing an old coat in the house. He wears it because it is the most comfortable garment he possesses, and home is the place for comfort.

Don't think it too much trouble to sing or play in an evening with your husband as sole audience. You couldn't have a more indulgent or appreciative one, as a general rule.

VI.—JEALOUSY

Don't be jealous of your husband's bachelor friends. Let him camp out with them for an occasional weekend if he wants to. He will come back all the fresher, and full of appreciation of his home.

Don't be jealous of your husband's acquaintance with other women. You don't want him to think you are the nicest woman in the world because he never sees any others, but because he sees plenty, and still feels that you are the only one in the world for him. Have nice girls about the house pretty frequently.

Don't give up all your men friends when you marry, and don't expect your husband to cease to take an interest in his women friends. Ask both to your home, and welcome them equally.

Don't try to excite your husband's jealousy by flirting with other men. You may succeed better than you want to. It is like playing with tigers and edged tools and volcanoes all in one.

Don't try too hard to regulate your husband's pleasures, and don't be jealous if they don't *always* include you.

Don't be jealous of your husband's club. If you are, he will go all the more. If you are perfectly willing for him to go as often as he likes, he would probably rather take you to the theatre.

Don't object to your husband cycling in to the country just because *you* don't cycle. If you can't, or mustn't, or don't want to, that's no reason for cutting off one of *his* chief pleasures.

Don't be jealous of your girl when she grows up because you are afraid you will have to take a back seat. Remain your daughter's companion, interested in all that interests her, and nobody will dream of drawing comparisons. She will never 'put your nose out of joint.'

Don't be jealous of your daughter's influence with her father. It won't undermine *yours* if you play your part properly. There is nothing more charming than the fellowship of a man and his budding daughter.

Don't be jealous of your husband's work. If he is any good, he is bound to be interested in it, and, after all, he is working for *you*.

Don't fill your heart with vain imaginings if your husband's business takes him away from you for weeks at a time. He is a good fellow, or you would not have married him. You must trust him; it is the essence of married life. But also—

Don't let him coop you up while he is away. You must live your life; you cannot vegetate. He must trust you. Any other attitude is an insult.

Don't forget the mountain and the molehill. Don't insist that your molehill is a mountain if you suspect your husband of flirting. There is no more certain way of making it into one. Your husband is only human, and if he is to be hanged, he would probably rather be hanged for a sheep than a lamb.

Don't be jealous, anyway. It belittles you, puts you at a disadvantage, and, if your husband thinks about it, is apt to make him unbearably conceited. Nothing makes you look old and worn sooner than jealousy, and nothing makes you more ridiculous.

VII.—RECREATION

Don't be afraid of being thought unfashionable if you go out with your husband; if you love each other, you will want to take your pleasures together as far as possible. On the other hand—

Don't object to your husband spending Saturday afternoons playing cricket because you can't play too. You can watch, or you can enjoy some pleasure that is not in his line, and it is advisable for him to have outdoor recreation.

Don't scoff at your husband as 'too old for tennis.' As long as he can play the game he is not too old for it.

Don't forget the anniversary of your wedding. Keep it up. The little celebration will draw you closer together year by year.

Don't think it is childish to celebrate birthdays. Your husband may not say anything, but he will carry an inward grievance if you forget the date. You need not buy expensive gifts, but let there be *something* special for him on that day. Ask his best friend to a nice little dinner, or arrange to dine in town together, and go to a theatre.

Don't refuse to take an interest in your husband's hobbies, but don't let him leave all the tiresome part of the work to you. If he loves to keep chickens, let him get up half an hour earlier in the morning to feed them. On the other hand, don't grudge a little help, and always be ready to sympathise about the broody hen or the fighting cockerel.

Don't encourage your husband to save money by pottering around at home during his holidays. It will do you both far more good to get a complete change of air and scene.

Don't insist on rushing about the Continent to see cities during your husband's summer holiday if he feels that a quiet rest by the sea, with a good golf-links handy, will be better for him. Never mind if you do get enough of the country; *he* doesn't, and you can run over to Paris for a week at some other time without wearing out your husband's nerves when they should be resting.

Don't say you can't go abroad if your husband wants to, because you don't like the Channel-crossing, and you hate foreign ways and foreign food. Subordinate your wishes to his for once, and you'll be surprised to find how much pleasure you pick up by the way.

Don't expect your husband always to share *your* recreations while you refuse to share his. If you like concerts best, and he prefers plays, let each sacrifice to the other in turn, and you will be surprised to find how your tastes become more catholic as time goes on.

Don't be afraid to rough it now and again with your husband as a companion. If he feels that he would like a week's walking tour with you as a chum, don't object that it may rain, or that you haven't a suitable dress, or that you can't manage for a week with nothing in the way of luggage except a nightdress and a tooth-brush. Enter into the spirit of the thing, and you'll get quite as much fun out of it as he will, and be happier than if he accompanied you to some fashionable resort where you would need to dress three or four times a day.

Don't take any notice of people who tell you constantly that a wife's place is in her husband's home, darning socks and stockings as women did in the good old days. You can darn all the socks and stockings there are to be darned, and you can be at home whenever your husband is, and very often when he is

not, and yet leave plenty of time for
going out.

Don't omit to fill your life with plenty
of outside interests. If you sing, join a
choral society; belong to a lecture or
literary society; keep up your French
and your music; visit your friends, and
invite them to visit you.   Nothing
induces dullness, and even illness, so
easily as lack of congenial occupation.
You will come back to your husband
with a bright face instead of a doleful
one.

Don't get into the habit of staying
indoors because there is nothing par-
ticular to go out for. Make an object if
you have not got one: take the dog for a
run on the common; walk to a shop two
miles away to match some wool—any-

thing to prevent the stay-at-home habit
from growing upon you.

Don't say you can't go out with your
husband because you can't leave the
children. Make arrangements that will
enable you to leave them in satisfactory
hands.

Don't refuse to run up to town for a
couple of days, when your husband has
to go on business, on the plea that you
have 'nothing to wear.' Go in what
you've got, and have a good time.

Don't object to your husband getting
a motor-bicycle; merely insist that he
shall buy a side-car for you at the same
time.

Don't say that golf is a selfish game,
and a married man ought to give it up.

You learn to play, and then join a mixed
club; your husband will be only too
delighted to have you with him. But
don't make up your mind that you could
never like the game until you've tried it.
Never mind if you don't become a crack
player; the main thing is to derive
pleasure from community of interest.

VIII.—FOOD

Don't forget to 'feed the brute' well.
Much depends on the state of his
digestion.

Don't talk to your husband about anything of a worrying nature until he has
finished his evening meal.

Don't buy expensive food, and have it

ruined in the cooking. If your cook isn't up to French dishes, be satisfied with English ones cooked to perfection.

Don't let your cook persist in frying steak when your husband likes it grilled, or in serving his eggs hard-boiled when he likes them milky.

Don't be afraid of cold meat. A few cookery lessons, or even a good cookery-book, with the use of a little intelligence, will make you mistress of delicious ways of serving up 'left overs'. Some men like it, but cold mutton has wrecked many happy homes.

Don't persist in having mushrooms on the table when you know they always make your husband ill. They may be *your* favourite dish, but is it worth it?

Don't give your husband burnt porridge. It is not enough to supply a double saucepan; you must see that it is regularly used.

Don't keep a servant who can't be punctual with meals. Nothing upsets a hungry man's temper more than being kept waiting for his dinner.

Don't let breakfast be a 'snatch' meal. Your husband often does the best part of his day's work on it, and the engine can't work if you don't stoke it properly.

Don't be careless about the way in which meals are served when you and your husband are alone. Dainty surroundings do much to make eating an agreeable process, instead of a mere means of keeping oneself alive.

Don't despise trifles. When two people make a home, the happiness of that home depends on trifles. For instance—

Don't despise the domestic potato. There are a hundred appetising ways of cooking it; but unless you take it firmly in hand, it will arrive at table with the consistency of half-melted ice—mushy without, stony within. The boiled potato is the rock on which many a happy home barque has foundered.

Don't give your husband stale bread if he prefers it new, nor new bread if it produces indigestion. Exercise a little thought in the matter.

Don't let your husband off the carving of the joint because he doesn't like doing it or does it badly. You have plenty of other things to do, and, besides, you don't want to show him up as a helpless man.

IX.—DRESS.

Don't take your husband on a laborious shopping expedition, and expect him to remain good-tempered throughout. If you want his advice on some special dress purchase, arrange to attend to that first, and then let him off. Men, as a rule, hate indiscriminate shopping.

Don't let your husband get into the habit of never noticing when you wear a new gown. Some men would be none the wiser if their wives wore sackcloth and ashes, but it is very discouraging to the wives.

Don't let your husband feel that it is a matter of indifference to you if he wears his socks wrong side out, or odd boots on his feet. Some men are absent-minded enough even for this; and if they can't keep a valet, their wives should see that they dress properly.

Don't let your husband wear a violet tie with grass-green socks. If he is unhappily devoid of the colour sense, he must be forcibly restrained, but—

Don't be sarcastic about your husband's taste in dress. Be gently persuasive and train his sense of fitness.

Don't impose your ideas on your husband in matters of individual taste so long as his style is not bad. He has a right to his own views.

Don't be induced to wear tailor-mades if they don't suit you just because your husband notices how well they suit so many other women. Probably you know best what suits *you*. But, on the other hand—

Don't reject your husband's advice on matters of dress without good reason. Many men have excellent taste and original ideas on the subject.

Don't think your husband extravagant because he pays more for his clothes than your brothers or your friends' husbands do. He pays for the cut as well as the material, and think how you would like to have your gowns made by a third-rate dressmaker.

Don't run away with the idea that it doesn't take a man as long to dress as a woman, and then be surprised that he keeps you waiting. Valet him yourself if you want him to be ready in time.

Don't dress badly, even if your allowance is small. If you can't have new gowns with every fleeting change of fashion, never have them made in an extreme style, so that they may not be too accurately dated. Let them be of good material, dainty, and well cut; there is nothing gained by being dowdy.

Don't allow yourself to get into the habit of dressing carelessly when there is 'only' your husband to see you. Depend upon it he has no use for faded tea-gowns and badly dressed hair, and he abhors the sight of curling pins as much as other men do. He is a man after all, and if his wife does not take the trouble to charm him, there are plenty of other women who will.

X.—ENTERTAINING.

Don't refuse to entertain your husband's friends on the ground that it is a 'bother'. Nothing pains a man more than finding only a cold welcome when he brings home a chum.

Don't be slavishly wedded to the dinner for dinner principle in entertaining. If you are, you must, of course, refuse all invitations which you cannot return in kind. But, after all, your friends are not really starving, and if some other form of entertaining suits you better, why be so hide-bound? Friendship is not a matter of bargaining.

Don't worry about getting into the 'very best' Society—with a big capital 'S'—afforded by your town or suburb. If the aristocratic inhabitants don't call on you, or the wealthy ones think you are not rich enough, it is not a matter to trouble you. A few friends are worth a host of acquaintances, and most of the really nice people will find you out.

Don't let visitors who are staying in the house feel themselves in the way. Give them the run of the place; don't shut them up in state in the drawing room.

Don't try to 'amuse' your guests every minute of the day. If they feel thoroughly at home, the amusement will come naturally. Don't forget to have books in every room.

Don't refuse to entertain at all because you can't do it on the same scale as your neighbours. The 'jolly little party' is generally preferred to the starchy reception.

Don't refuse to adapt yourself to the style of entertaining which is first favourite in your locality. If you are thrown amongst a non musical set of people, it is not the least use inviting them to be miserable at a musical evening. If, on the other hand, your lot is cast amongst a set that despises cards, it is hopeless to issue invitations for a bridge-party.

Don't say you can't give progressive bridge-parties because you can't afford to buy expensive prizes. Make up for it in the care with which you select them; let them be good of their kind and unpretentious, and you will find the lucky winners quite as pleased with your prize as an elaborate one won elsewhere, which cost as many pounds as yours cost shillings.

Don't feel worried because you can't afford to offer your friends a champagne supper. They can be just as jolly on claret-cup, and will think none the less of you for keeping within your means.

Don't in any case try to entertain in a way that is beyond your means just because other people do it.

XI.—HOUSEHOLD MANAGE-
MENT.

Don't sneer at your mother's old-fashioned ways. They suited your father well enough, and perhaps she can give you points.

Don't sneer at your mother in law's old fashioned ways; you may hurt your husband as well as his mother.

Don't think anything too much trouble to do for your husband's comfort; remember he is occupied all day in working for *you*. Don't be afraid of thinking and planning and working for *him*.

Don't think your household gods of more importance than your husband's comfort. Don't for instance refuse to give him a bedroom fire in cold weather because it makes 'too much dust.'

Don't keep the house so tidy that your husband is afraid to leave a newspaper lying about. Few men have such a sense of order as most women have, and they are naturally more careless at home than at the office. But what does it matter when you really come to think of it?

Don't quarrel with your husband's relatives. If you can't get on with them, don't ask them to visit you, but persuade your husband to visit *them* occasionally. As a rule, however, a little tact and patience will carry you over the thin ice.

Don't allow outsiders to interfere in your household management. Even mothers should lie low, but—

Don't refuse to listen to good advice from people of experience, and act upon it if you can.

Don't get angry if your husband says that he never now tastes cake like that his mother used to make. Write and ask her for the recipe.

Don't become too stereotyped to try new methods that may be better than the old ones.

Don't let the house get stuffy by sitting with closed windows. Keep the air moving, and let your husband come home to a healthy atmosphere in more than one sense.

Don't let fashionable wives persuade you to give up your home and live in hotels or boarding-houses. It may be less troublesome for you, but it is also less comfortable, and infinitely less pleasing to the average man. If you've got a home of your own, stick to it and be happy in it. You don't want to live your lives in public.

Don't forget your poorer neighbours. If every family that had enough to eat kept an eye on even one family that hadn't, there would be much less misery in the country.

Don't omit to oil the wheels of the domestic machinery so that they don't annoy your husband by running badly. If you can't keep your servants in a good temper, change them. Don't make things uncomfortable by scolding them in your husbands' presence for sins of omission and commission. In fact, keep the machinery in the background as much as possible, letting him see only the results. But—

Don't forget that your husband is your chum and will be delighted to be called upon in an emergency. Your young husband will like to save you by lighting the early morning fire when you are 'in a hole.'

Don't have a 'spring cleaning' any oftener than your special nature renders absolutely necessary. Some women have at least four every year. When you do have one, don't upset the whole house at once. Men hate to find a place in disorder, and if you take one room at a time, your husband need know very little about it except when workmen are required.

Don't have your husband's den turned upside down once a week, and everything put back into a different place. When the necessary amount of sweeping and dusting has been done, replace everything as nearly as possible in the position in which he left it, even if it is not quite 'tidy.' You can be tidy in your own part of the house to make up for it.

Don't be afraid of soiling your hands if it be necessary. There is nothing undignified about housework, and if circumstances make it necessary or advisable for you to do it, do it to the very best of your ability. Besides, it's a good thing to be able to feel that you never expect anything of your servants that you couldn't do for yourself if it were expedient.

Don't permit yourself to forget for a single instant that nothing is more annoying to a tired man than the sight of a half-finished laundry work. The remotest hint in your home of a 'washing day' is like a red rag to a bull.

Don't get up at six every morning, and don't expect your husband to do it either, to see if the maids are stirring. When you engage a servant, explain that you expect her to rely upon herself for getting up to time. Send her to bed in good time. Give her a reliable clock and let her take the responsibility.

Don't be a household martyr. Some wives are never happy unless they are miserable, but their husbands don't appreciate this peculiar trait. The woeful smile is most exasperating.

Don't let your servants use paraffin for fire-lighting purposes, nor leave a newspaper fastened up in front of the fireplace to 'draw up' the fire. If you do, they will probably have your house set on fire some time or other.

Don't say it's a waste of time to make marmalade at home when you can get it better made from the stores. Your husband and children never like *any* so well as yours, and it is worth the trouble of making to see how they enjoy eating it.

Don't omit to learn how to put on a bandage. You will be very lucky if you get through your married life without having to do it for some member of the family, and the right way is so much better than the wrong one.

Don't forget to reduce the housework to a minimum by abolishing all *unnecessary* polishing of metal, washing of curtains and sweeping of carpets.

Don't swathe all your chairs and couches in covers while they look nice and fresh. Time enough for that when they become shabby. Furniture wrappers banish the 'homey' feeling.

Don't arrange for the chimney sweep to come on the day your husband

Originally published 1913

Republished 2007
by A & C Black,
Bloomsbury Publishing PLC
50 Bedford Square,
London
WC1B 3DP

www.bloomsbury.com

Bloomsbury is a registered trademark of
Bloomsbury Publishing Plc

ISBN 9780713687903

A CIP catalogue record for this book is available
from the British Library.

Printed by WKT Company Ltd, China

29 30 28

there is nothing derogatory to his dignity in handling him.

Don't give baby the same name as his father, and then have to talk of 'Big John' and 'Little John', or of 'Old John' and 'Young John'. Call your husband always by his own name, and let your boys have names of their own too.

Don't grudge the years you spend on child-bearing and child-rearing. Remember you are training future citizens, and it is the most important mission in the world.